Raintree is an imprint of Capstone Global Library Limited, a company incorporated in England and Wales having its registered office at 7 Pilgrim Street, London, EC4V 6LB – Registered company number: 6695582

To contact Raintree please phone 0845 6044371, fax + 44 (0) 1865 312263, or email myorders@ raintreepublishers.co.uk. Customers from outside the UK please telephone +44 1865 312262.

Text © Capstone Global Library Limited 2013
First published in hardback in 2013
Paperback edition first published in 2014
The moral rights of the proprietor have been asserted.

Edited by Rebecca Rissman, Daniel Nunn, and Adrian Vigliano
Designed by Cynthia Della-Rovere
Picture research by Elizabeth Alexander
Production by Alison Parsons
Originated by Capstone Global Library Ltd
Printed and bound in China by China Translation and Printing Services Ltd

ISBN 978 1 406 25104 3 (hardback)
16 15 14 13 12
10 9 8 7 6 5 4 3 2 1

ISBN 978 1 406 25111 1 (paperback)
17 16 15 14 13
10 9 8 7 6 5 4 3 2 1

British Library Cataloguing in Publication Data
Labrecque, Ellen.
Crazy stunts. -- (Try this at home!)
790.1-dc23
A full catalogue record for this book is available from the British Library.

Acknowledgements
We would like to thank the following for permission to reproduce photographs: Alamy pp. 4 (© Radius Images), 5 (© Filmstore collection Ltd), 28 (© Science Photo Library/Ian Boddy); © Capstone Publishers pp. 6, 8 t, 8 b, 9 t, 9 b, 10, 11 t, 11 b, 12 t, 12 b, 13 t, 13 b, 14, 15 t, 15 b, 16, 17, 18, 19, 20, 21, 22, 23, 24, 25 t, 25 b, 26 t, 26 b, 27 t, 27 b (Karon Dubke); Getty Images pp. 7 (Jason Merritt/FilmMagic), 29 (Stuart Morton/WireImage). Design features reproduced with the permission of Shutterstock (© Nelson Marques), (© Tajne), (© Alex Staroseltsev), (© Merve Poray), (© Nicemonkey).

Cover photograph of teenage boys fighting reproduced with permission of Getty Images (Laure LIDJI/ StockImage).

Every effort has been made to contact copyright holders of material reproduced in this book. Any omissions will be rectified in subsequent printings if notice is given to the publisher.

All the internet addresses (URLs) given in this book were valid at the time of going to press. However, due to the dynamic nature of the internet, some addresses may have changed, or sites may have changed or ceased to exist since publication. While the author and publisher regret any inconvenience this may cause readers, no responsibility for any such changes can be accepted by either the author or the publisher.

ADMIT ONE
371416
371416

Don't Try This At Home!

Crazy Stunts

Ellen Labrecque

Raintree

Contents

Some words are shown in bold, **like this**. You can find out what they mean by looking in the Glossary.

What are stunts?

Do you like watching amazing stunts in films? Do you want to pull off stunts in your own films or shows? Wow your friends by floating into the air or throwing a fierce (but fake!) punch? How about fooling your friends into believing you are ill?

But, *shhhh*! Don't share these secrets with your friends. After all, you don't want them to know how you pull off these stunts. You just want them to be amazed!

Be safe

Pulling off stunts can be exciting. Just ask the **stunt people** in films, who climb and leap off tall buildings. But when they do stunts on camera, safety is their number-one concern. It should be yours, too.

When you do a stunt, do it slowly and carefully at first. If you are doing your stunt with another person, make sure they know what to expect. Nobody should be surprised if they are supposed to be part of a stunt.

Rise up!

STEP **1**

Want to look like you are rising off the ground? Stand with your legs together and your left side facing your audience.

STEP **2**

Without letting them see, slide your foot out of your right shoe. Angle your foot so your heel is pressing against the back of the empty shoe.

STEP 3

Use your right foot and press against the shoe to lift it up. At the same time, lift your left leg off the ground. Your left foot and your right shoe "rise" together.

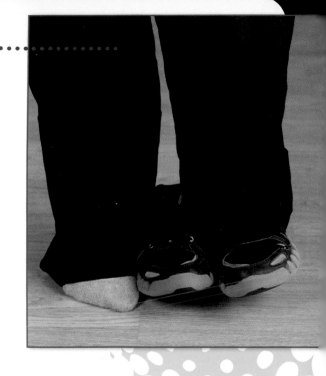

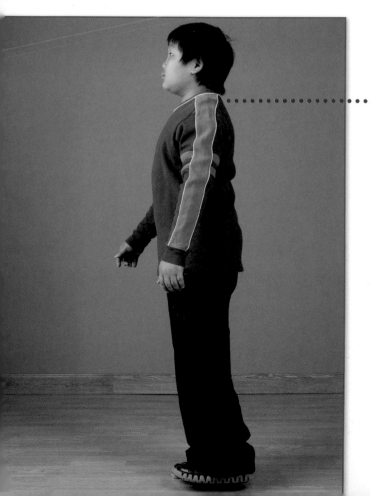

STEP 4

After a few seconds of "**levitating**", put both shoes back on the ground. Slip your right foot slyly back into your shoe again. Ta-da!

Fall over

STEP 1

Sometimes it's fun to make friends think you are clumsy. Here's how to fall over safely and look silly. As you walk, step one foot in front of the other. Walk quickly so your fall will look even more real.

STEP 2

Raise one foot to take the next step. Bump the raised foot into your other foot on the ankle or calf and twist it around the leg.

STEP 3

Try this on soft grass or cushions first!

Fall forward and brace your fall with your arms. Bring yourself down as softly as possible.

Fake throwing up

STEP 1...

You can pull off being sick without fake vomit. First, slump into a chair and say you feel dizzy and weak.

STEP 2

Tell your friends that your tummy hurts.

12

STEP 3

At just the right moment, say you are going to the bathroom.

STEP 4

Make loud gagging noises followed by retching. Dump a cup of water into the toilet.

Flush, wash your hands, and pretend to clean up. Walk out of the bathroom and yell "gotcha"! You also want to make sure your friends know you are not really sick.

Fake break your nose

STEP 1

Put your hands together with the tips of your fingers on the sides of your nose. Tuck in your thumbs so they are by your lips.

STEP 2

Put both thumb nails behind your front teeth. Act as if you are struggling to move your nose to the right side with your fingers.

STEP 3

When you finally move it, flick your thumbnails off the edges of your front teeth. This will make a cracking sound. Make a face as if it really hurt.

Watch as your friends look disgusted!

Fake a punch

STEP **1**

You'll need a friend to help you with this stunt. Face your partner and stand an arm's length apart. Make eye contact so your friend knows the "punch" is coming. Ball your right hand into a fist and cock your arm behind you.

STEP 2

Bring your other arm up in front
and keep your hand open.

STEP 3

Bring your hitting arm all the way around in a punching motion. Your fist will come in front of your partner's face.

ADMIT ONE

When it does, punch your other hand to make a loud hitting noise. At the same time as the fake punch is thrown, your friend should throw his head back like he just got hit.

STEP 4

Follow through with the punch all the way across your body. At first, go slowly and **exaggerate** the punching motion. As you gain confidence, you can punch faster.

Fake a kick

You'll need a partner to help with this stunt. Face your friend and stand an arm's length apart.

STEP 1

ADMIT ONE

Make eye contact so your friend knows the "kick" is coming.

Lift up your leg and kick up towards your partner's chest. Keep your left arm up to help you stay balanced on one foot as you kick.

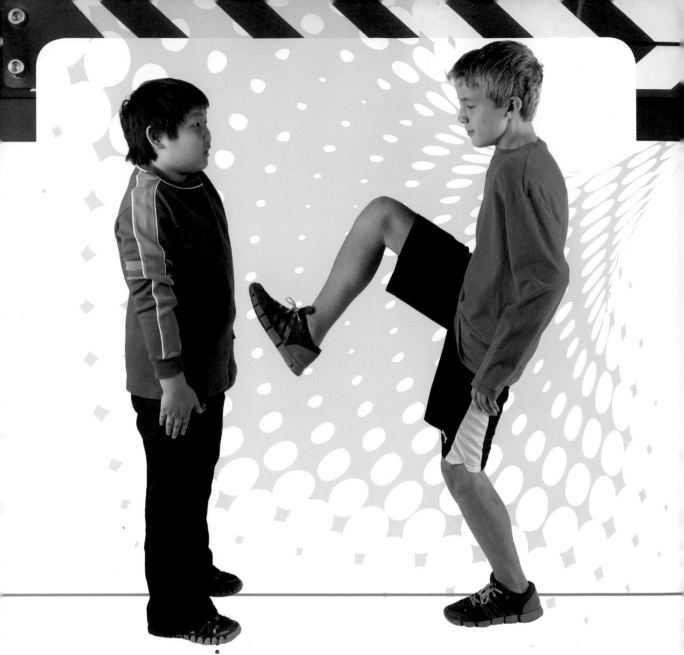

STEP 3

When your foot gets right in front of the chest, your partner should slap his leg to make a loud "whack" sound.

While your friend slaps his leg, he should fall back like he's been kicked. Pull your leg back down and stare at your friend like you are tough and ready to kick again.

Fake walk into a closed door

Casually walk towards the door. Whistling while you walk will make the stunt even funnier.

STEP 1

STEP 2

When you approach the door, kick the bottom of it with either foot to make a loud noise.

STEP 3

As you kick from the bottom, throw your head back like it just slammed into the door.

Stumble around like you are dizzy from hitting your head.

Eat your eyeball!

Level of difficulty: Medium

DIRECTOR

STEP 1

Put your right fingers over your right eye in a grabbing motion. Pretend to pull your eyeball out of the socket.

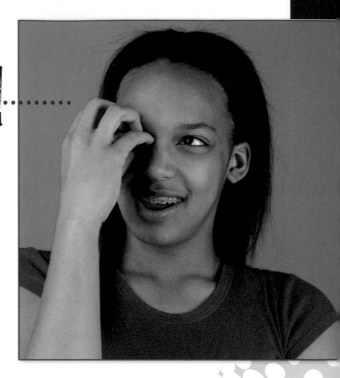

STEP 2

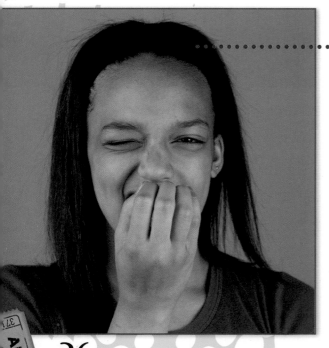

Close your eyelid straight afterwards. Keep your fingers closed like they are holding the eyeball and put them in front of your mouth.

STEP 3

Pretend to put the eyeball inside your mouth. Push your tongue back and forth from cheek to cheek to make it seem like you are moving it around.

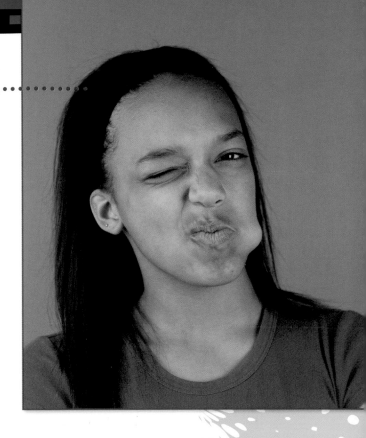

STEP 4

Finish the trick by making a giant swallowing motion. Bye-bye eyeball!

Sell your stunts

You don't "do" stunts. You **act** out the stunts to make them seem real. Here are five tips to help you do just that.

1. Set up the stunt. If you are going to fake punch somebody, make sure there is an argument before the punch.

2. Sound effects are a must – the louder, the better.

3. Use **distraction** as a tool.

4. Practise your stunts in front of a mirror. Then you'll know what looks good and what doesn't.

5. Don't share your secrets. The fewer people who know how to do it, the cooler it is!

Glossary

act pretend to do or be something that you are not

distraction something that draws away the mind or eyes from something else that is happening

exaggerate make something seem larger or more extreme

levitate rise up into the air

stunt people people who perform dangerous and athletic feats

Find out more

Books

Being a Stuntman (Radar), Isabel Thomas (Wayland, 2012)

Stunt Man (321 Go), Stephen Rickard (Ransom Publishing, 2010)

The World's Most Dangerous Stunts, Tim O'Shei (Capstone Publishing, 2006)

Websites

www.kidstube.com
Children can upload their own videos of themselves doing stunts!

www.stuntkids.com
A place you can look if you are serious about trying to do stunts for real.

www.timeforkids.com
This website reviews and talks about children's films that include first-rate stunts.

Index